big bowl

RYLAND
PETERS
& SMALL

Elsa Petersen-Schepelern

big bowl

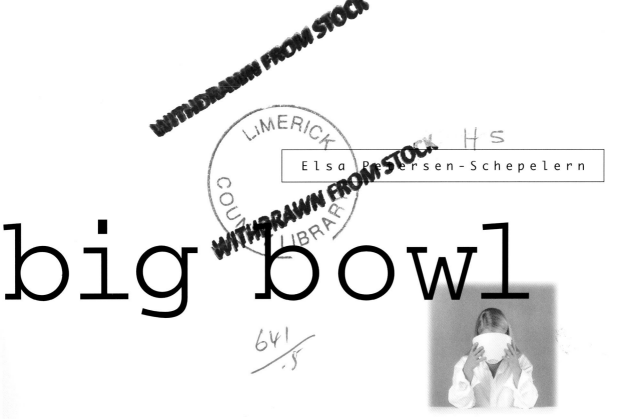

photography by Jeremy Hopley

Designer **Paul Tilby**
Editor **Elsa Petersen-Schepelern**
Creative Director **Jacqui Small**
Publishing Director **Anne Ryland**
Production **Meryl Silbert**
Food Stylist **Melina Keays**
Stylist **Page Marchese**
Photographer's Assistant **Catherine Rowlands**
Author Photograph **Francis Loney**

Acknowledgements
My thanks to my sister Kirsten, Luc Votan, Peter
Bray, Clare Ferguson, Sonia Stevenson, Nowelle
and Clemente Valentino-Capezza, Susan and Tim.
Thanks to Becky Johnson for her enthusiastic
and knowledgeable assistance and for helping
with recipe testing – and to the shoot team who
made the whole experience such fun.
My heartfelt thanks also to the ceramicists and
suppliers who lent us the beautiful bowls for
this book, including Egg, Livingstone Studio,
Oggetti, Maryse Boxer, Muji, Sue Paraskeva
and Divertimenti.

Notes
All spoon measurements are level unless
otherwise noted.
Ovens should be preheated to the specified
temperature. If using a fan oven, cooking
times should be reduced according to
manufacturer's instructions.

First published in Great Britain in 1998
by Ryland Peters & Small
Cavendish House, 51–55 Mortimer Street,
London W1N 7TD

Text © Elsa Petersen-Schepelern 1998
Design and photographs
© Ryland Peters & Small 1998

Produced by Toppan, Hong Kong
Printed and bound in China

ISBN 1 900518 53 8

A CIP record for this book is available from the
British Library

contents

introduction

These thirty recipes are just a few of my favourite casual dishes. I cook them as a quick meal-in-a-bowl when I'm by myself, or in larger quantities when friends and colleagues drop over for a casual lunch or dinner. If you increase the quantities, many of these dishes can be prepared in bulk for parties, when people need a little sustenance to help the conversation swing. In fact, they're so versatile I also find they can be adapted for more formal occasions – the sort of dinner party when I'm playing ladies! The only difference is that the bowls need to be a little more formal than for the more casual 'dinner-in-front-of-the-fire' kind of event.

Every cuisine seems to have dishes suitable for the Big Bowl treatment. My own passions are for fresh-tasting Asian dishes, just packed with spice and flavour – or for comforting European food from the 'Cuisine Grandmere' school of thought.

Choose the size of bowl that suits your appetite – mine is enormous in winter and only a little less enthusiastic in summer. You'll soon find which of these categories applies to you. Be assured, these recipes are not for birdlike appetites!

singapore laksa

Laksas are found in different forms all over the Malay peninsula. In Penang they are almost overpoweringly fishy, while in Singapore they can be very spicy – this version is milder. You can vary the ingredients according to what's available in the market, and to suit your own taste: but the basics should be a truly wonderful, flavourful stock, plus noodles. I like Japanese somen noodles, but fine cellophane noodles are probably more common. The spice paste can also be simplified by using one of the ready-made Thai pastes instead.

2 tablespoons corn or peanut oil

500 ml coconut milk

500 ml boiling fish or chicken stock

1 cooked chicken breast, shredded

2 fried Chinese fishcakes, sliced (optional)

12 uncooked prawns (optional)

200 g somen or cellophane noodles, soaked according to packet instructions

6 spring onions

1 bunch of coriander

4 handfuls of beansprouts, trimmed

1 bunch of mint or Vietnamese mint

spice paste

3 stalks lemongrass, sliced

4 garlic cloves, sliced

2.5 cm fresh ginger, peeled and sliced

3 shallots or 6 Thai shallots, chopped

4 candlenuts or 8 blanched almonds

3 red chillies, deseeded

1 teaspoon turmeric

1 teaspoon salt

1 teaspoon sugar, preferably brown

serves 4

Grind all the spice paste ingredients in a spice grinder or blender, adding a little oil if necessary. Heat the oil in a wok and fry the paste for 6–8 minutes without burning. Add the coconut milk and stock and simmer gently for 5 minutes to develop the flavours. Add the chicken, fishcakes and prawns, if using, and simmer for 2 minutes or until the prawns become opaque. Prepare the noodles according to the packet instructions. Share the noodles, chicken, fishcakes, prawns, spring onions, coriander, beansprouts and mint between 4 big bowls. Pour over the coconut stock and serve.

soups

thai mussel soup

with coconut milk and lemongrass

A Thai version of the French classic, moules à la marinière. Most mussels sold by fish shops have been farmed, and seem to need less cleaning than wild ones. In any case, you should scrub the shells with a small brush and either pull off or cut off the 'beards'. Use mussels that are tightly closed – tap any open ones against your worktop, and discard them if they still don't close. Steam the mussels open, discarding any that stay closed. When you buy mussels, keep them cool and use them the same day. The best mussel-eating implement is an empty pair of shells – use them as pincers to nip the others out of their shells.

To make the coconut stock, put the lemongrass, ginger, lime leaves and garlic in a small food processor and work to a smooth paste. Heat the oil in a saucepan, add the paste and chillies, and stir-fry until you cough. Add the fish stock, bring to the boil, and simmer 5–10 minutes to extract the flavours. Add the coconut milk and heat to simmering.

Chop 1 stalk lemongrass into a large pan with the fish stock or water and boil briskly. Add the mussels, one layer at a time, and cook until they open, transferring them to 4 big bowls as they do.

Strain the coconut stock over the mussels. Scatter with sliced chillies, lime zest and coriander and serve immediately, with another empty bowl to take the discarded shells.

Be prepared to double the quantity of mussels because your guests will love this dish!

1 stalk lemongrass

250 ml fish stock or water

2–3 bags mussels, about 1 kg each

coconut stock

3 stalks lemongrass, chopped

2.5 cm fresh ginger, peeled and sliced

6 kaffir lime leaves, snipped

3 garlic cloves, sliced

1–2 tablespoons corn oil

1–2 red chillies, sliced

500 ml fish stock

500 ml coconut milk

to serve

2 red chillies, finely sliced

grated zest of 3 kaffir limes

sprigs of coriander

serves 4

chinese treasure soup

I always buy Chinese barbecued duck and pork, but you can make your own by rubbing with chilli oil or honey and 5-spice, then roasting or grilling. Other treasures can be added to taste, including wontons of minced pork, fish balls or pork balls, and other Chinese vegetables such as bok choy, pea shoots, lotus root and bamboo shoots. The usual number of treasures is the magical eight.

Heat the duck and pork in the oven at 200°C (400°F) Gas Mark 6 until hot. (If cooking your own duck or pork, see the note below.)

To make the wontons, mix the minced pork, bamboo shoots and salt in a bowl. Put 1 tablespoon of mixture in the middle of each wonton skin and brush a circle of egg white around it. Twirl the wonton skin around the filling to make a shuttlecock shape.

Put all the stock ingredients in a saucepan and simmer for 30 minutes to meld the flavours. Strain out the solids and return the stock to the rinsed pan. Return the stock to the boil and add the carrot and wontons , Simmer for 3–5 minutes until the wontons rise to the surface and the filling is cooked.

Put the prawns, beancurd, cabbage and wontons in 4 big bowls, then pour over the boiling stock. Add the beansprouts, shredded duck and pork, and serve with chopsticks and Chinese spoons.

Note: If using char-grilled duck, rub 1 duck breast with 5-spice powder and honey. Heat a stove-top grill-pan and cook, skin side down, until the fat begins to run. Pour off the fat at intervals, and continue cooking for about 20 minutes until the skin is crispy. Turn it over and cook the other side until brown – the centre will remain pink. Set aside to set the juices then cut crossways into 1 cm slices.

If cooking your own pork, brush with chilli oil and roast at 240°C (475°F) Gas Mark 9 until very crisp. Set aside to set the juices, then slice into bite-sized pieces.

½ Chinese barbecued duck, shredded

1 piece of Chinese barbecued pork spareribs, about 15 cm square, chopped into bite-sized pieces (optional)

1 carrot, scored lengthways, then finely sliced

6 uncooked prawns, shelled but with tail fins intact

2 sticks fried beancurd, sliced

2 leaves Chinese cabbage, sliced

a handful of fresh beansprouts, trimmed

wontons

250 g minced pork

3 canned bamboo shoots, chopped

a pinch of salt

12 wonton skins

1 egg white, beaten

chinese stock

2 litres chicken stock

4 star anise

10 cm fresh ginger, peeled and finely sliced

1 onion, sliced

serves 4

Japanese noodle soups are amazingly quick and easy. The smoked fish used here can be replaced by any number of other ingredients, such as cooked chicken, barbecued pork, finely sliced beef or blanched vegetables. Just make sure the pieces are bite-sized for easy chopstick-wielding. Dashi, the delicious Japanese stock that smells of the sea, is made from seaweed and grated bonito, a species of tuna, and sold as powder or liquid concentrate in some of the larger supermarkets, as well as Asian shops.

japanese noodle soup

with seaweed and smoked fish

2 packets Japanese noodles (udon, ramen, somen or soba)

500 g smoked haddock or cod, skinned and cut in 4 squares

1 litre dashi stock (see recipe introduction)

1 small packet dried wakame seaweed (optional)

4 spring onions, finely sliced diagonally

Japanese 7-spice powder – shichimi togarishi (optional)

to serve

wasabi paste

Japanese soy sauce

serves 4

Prepare the noodles according to the packet instructions. Drain, then put into cold water.

Put the fish in a bowl, then pour over boiling water. Leave for 2 minutes, then drain (if you like, the liquid may be used to make the stock, but the stock will then be a little cloudy).

Heat the stock, add the wakame seaweed, reheat to boiling, then add the fish and drained noodles and reheat to boiling point.

Serve immediately, sprinkled with the sliced spring onions and Japanese 7-spice powder, if using. Serve separate small dishes of wasabi paste and another of soy sauce.

pho bo - vietnamese beef noodle soup

2 packets fresh *ho-fun* noodles or 4 bundles dried *banh pho* broad rice noodles

1 onion, finely sliced

1–4 hot red chillies, deseeded and finely sliced

125 g rump or fillet steak, very finely sliced (freezing it first makes it easier to slice)

2 tablespoons lime or lemon juice

1 bunch of fresh coriander

1 bunch of Vietnamese basil, sliced (do not use European – omit if you can't find Asian)

1 bunch of Vietnamese mint

1 lime, quartered

75 ml *nuoc mam* (Vietnamese fish sauce), to serve

Vietnamese beef stock

3 litres beef stock

3–4 onions, finely sliced

2.5 cm fresh ginger, sliced

8 star anise

½ lemon or lime, with rind

1 tablespoon fish sauce

1 teaspoon sugar

serves 4

My Vietnamese nephew is, I'm irritated to have to admit, the very best cook in our family. He moved to Australia as a student, and had to learn to cook very fast indeed. He has contributed many breathtakingly wonderful dishes to our family repertoire, and this is just one of them. In Vietnam, salt is not served at the table, so all dishes must be seasoned when they are being cooked. Luc uses fresh ho-fun noodles, sold folded into book-sized packs, soft, moist and ready to use. Mostly they are sold ready-cut, but if not you cut them into 1 cm strips. If you want to make the beef stock from scratch, use about 2 kg beef bones and 750 g stewing steak and simmer with the onions and spices for about 4 hours. I'm lazy, so I give the easier cheat's method!

First flavour the beef stock by simmering it in a saucepan with the remaining stock ingredients for about 15 minutes. If using dried noodles, put them into a bowl and cover with hot water. Let soak for 30 minutes, then refresh in cold water. Leave in cold water until ready to serve. If using ho-fun noodles, carefully cut or separate them into strips.

Simmer the onion in boiling water for 2 minutes (or microwave for 2 minutes). Dip the noodles briefly in boiling water until hot, then divide between 4 big bowls. Add the onions and chillies, then the beef on top. Pour over the boiling stock, then add the lemon or lime juice and herbs. Serve with wedges of lime, a separate bowl of nuoc mam (Vietnamese fish sauce – you can use Thai instead if you like), chopsticks and a optional tablespoon so you don't slurp too loudly!

Two classic Tuscan soups for the price of one recipe – serve it the day it's made, or the next day after reboiling – 'ribollita'. The lettuce added at the end isn't traditional, but I like the extra crunch!

tuscan ribollita

Soak the beans 4–6 hours in cold water to cover. Drain, then put into a saucepan with the onion wedges, quartered carrot and half the garlic, cover with water, bring to the boil and simmer until done (the time will depend on the age of the beans, but reckon on about 1 hour).

Drain and remove the flavourings, then put half the beans in a food processor and zap to a rough purée. Press through a mouli or potato ricer to remove the bits of bean skin.

Put about 4 tablespoons of the olive oil in a saucepan, add the sliced onion and cook until soft and translucent. Add the chilli and remaining garlic and cook for about 5 minutes more. Add the tomatoes and puréed beans, plus salt and freshly ground black pepper. Cook for about 5 minutes, then add the leek, celery, thyme, potatoes, remaining carrots and cabbage. Bring to the boil and simmer until the vegetables are done – about 20 minutes.

Add the whole beans, season to taste, reheat and serve immediately or set aside until the next day for ribollita.

To make the ribollita, first reheat the soup. Rub the toast with the garlic butter and put into 4 big bowls. Add the lettuce, ladle the soup over the top and drizzle with a little olive oil. Sprinkle with parsley, then serve.

250 g dried cannellini beans

2 onions (1 cut in 4 wedges through the root, and 1 sliced)

3 carrots (1 cut into quarters lengthways, and 2 sliced)

6 garlic cloves, smashed

6 tablespoons extra-virgin olive oil, plus extra for drizzling

1 fresh chilli, deseeded and sliced

250 g tomatoes, skinned and chopped

1 leek, sliced

2 celery stalks, finely diced

sprigs of thyme

3 waxy potatoes, cubed

1 Savoy cabbage (or *cavalo nero*), sliced

sea salt and freshly ground black pepper

ribollita

8 slices ciabatta bread, toasted

4 tablespoons butter, mashed with 1 crushed garlic clove

1 cos lettuce, sliced

4 tablespoons chopped parsley (optional)

serves 4

There are many versions of the classic Caesar Salad - the archetypal meal for Ladies Who Lunch. The remarkable Julia Child says anchovies weren't used in the original, but Worcestershire sauce was (and that contains anchovies). It also included a one-minute egg, but like so many wonderful things, this would be regarded as unsafe these days, and I have included a soft-cooked 4-minute egg. I do love her recommendation for serving the leaves whole - dip them into the dressing and eat them with your fingers, then eat the croutons with a fork.

caesar salad

1 small head young cos lettuce

2 tablespoons extra-virgin olive oil

½ tablespoon lemon juice, plus 1 lemon, cut in wedges

sea salt flakes and freshly ground black pepper

croutons

1 thick slice challah bread, brioche or other white bread

oil and/or butter, for frying

1 large garlic clove, smashed

to serve

3–4 rinsed anchovy fillets

1 soft-cooked (4-minute) medium-sized egg, peeled and halved or quartered

Parmesan cheese, shaved into curls with a vegetable peeler

serves 1

To make the croutons, toast the slice of bread or brioche lightly. Cut into big cubes, cutting off and discarding the crusts. Heat the oil and butter in a pan and add the garlic clove. Add the cubes of bread and cook, turning, until golden on all sides. Discard the garlic after about 1 minute – do not let it burn. When the cubes are golden, remove and drain on kitchen paper.

Put the lettuce in a large bowl and sprinkle with olive oil. Using your hands, roll the leaves in the oil. Sprinkle with lemon juice and roll again.

Divide the croutons between 4 big bowls and put the dressed whole leaves on top. Sprinkle with salt and lots of freshly ground black pepper. Add the anchovies, egg and shavings of Parmesan and serve.

Note: If you don't like anchovies, omit them, and add 1 teaspoon Worcestershire sauce to the dressing.

salads

blue cheese salad

with crispy pancetta and pine nuts

This salad of herb sprigs and mixed leaves - peppery, soft and bitter - is dressed with a creamy blue cheese dressing. It's suitable for a first course, a salad course after the meat, or as a big-bowl lunch, as here.

2 tablespoons pine nuts

1 tablespoon olive oil, for frying

8–12 slices smoked pancetta

125 g Dolcellate, Gorgonzola or other blue cheese, diced

3 tablespoons extra-virgin olive oil, or to taste

1 tablespoon white rice vinegar or lemon juice, or to taste

mixed salad leaves, including peppery leaves like watercress and mustard, bitter ones like frisée, soft ones like mignonette or butter lettuce, and herb sprigs like rocket

1 avocado, scooped into balls with a teaspoon (optional)

sea salt flakes and freshly ground black pepper

serves 4

Put the pine nuts in a dry pan and fry for about 1–2 minutes only, until golden. Set aside.

Heat the olive oil in the pan, add the pancetta and fry until crispy. Transfer to a plate lined with kitchen paper to drain.

Put the cheese in the bottom of a large salad bowl and crumble well with a fork. Add the extra-virgin olive oil and vinegar or lemon juice, Mash, then beat to a loose and creamy consistency. Add lots of freshly ground black pepper and salt to taste.

Put the salad leaves on top of the cheese dressing, then add the avocado, if using. Sprinkle with the pancetta and pine nuts (scrape any crunchy bits from the pan into the bowl too).

Serve, in the salad bowl, for guests to help themselves, or make in 4 big bowls, dividing the ingredients as appropriate. Lots of wine and some crusty bread are the perfect accompaniments.

There are as many variations of this Tuscan bread salad as there are cooks.

panzanella

The trick is to let the flavours blend well without allowing the bread to disintegrate into a mush. The key is to use the ripest, reddest, most flavourful tomatoes you can find ('marmande' are my favourite).

6 very ripe plum tomatoes

2 garlic cloves

4 thick slices day-old bread, preferably Italian-style

½ cucumber, halved, deseeded and finely sliced diagonally

1 red onion, diced

1 tablespoons chopped parsley

8–12 tablespoons extra-virgin olive oil

2 tablespoons white rice vinegar

1 teaspoon balsamic vinegar (optional)

1 bunch of basil leaves, torn

12 caperberries, or to taste (optional)

sea salt and freshly ground black pepper

serves 4

Cut the tomatoes in half, spike with slivers of garlic and roast in the oven at 200°C (400°F) Gas Mark 6 for about 1 hour until wilted and some of the moisture has evaporated.

Meanwhile, tear the bread into pieces and put in bowl. Sprinkle with a little water until damp. Add the tomatoes, cucumber, onion, parsley, salt and pepper. Sprinkle with the olive oil and vinegar, toss well, then set aside for about 1 hour to develop the flavours. Add the basil and caperberries and serve.

Variation: Toast the slices of bread under the grill or cook on a char-grill before tearing into pieces.

There is much debate about the correct ingredients for this salad. Some experts say all the vegetables should be raw, others not. Usually, tinned tuna would be used, but modern cooks have improved upon what was already a perfect dish by char-grilling the tuna until rare. Another wonderful method is to stew it gently in olive oil for 30-45 minutes. Substitute as you like.

salade niçoise

500 g Chinese snake beans, green beans or sugarsnap peas

125 g shelled broad beans

2 orange, red or yellow peppers (optional)

1 thick slice fresh tuna, about 500 g

4 tablespoons extra-virgin olive oil, plus extra, for brushing

4 teaspoons white rice vinegar

mixed salad leaves, to taste

8 cherry tomatoes, halved

12–20 black Provençal olives

4 soft-boiled (4-minute) eggs (optional)

sprigs of basil (optional)

4–8 anchovy fillets, rinsed (optional)

salt and freshly ground black pepper

serves 4

If using snake beans, cut them in to 7 cm lengths. Cook the beans in boiling salted water until just al dente, then refresh in iced water. Pat dry.

Cook the broad beans in boiling salted water until tender. Cool quickly in iced water, then drain and pop them out of their grey skins. Prepare the peppers, if using (see note).

Brush the tuna with 1 tablespoon olive oil, then char-grill on a stove-top grill pan until crisp outside and pink inside. Remove and cut into 1 cm slices.

Divide the remaining oil, rice vinegar, salt and pepper between 4 big bowls and beat with a fork. Add the salad leaves and toss well. Add the beans, tomatoes, olives and tuna slices. Cut the eggs, if using, into quarters and add to the bowls. Top with basil and anchovy fillets, if using, sea salt flakes and lots of freshly ground black pepper.

Note: To skin the peppers, char them over a flame or under the grill. Scrape off the burned skin and slice the flesh. I love the taste of charred peppers, but it's not traditional. If serving raw peppers, I prefer to peel them with a vegetable peeler, then core and slice into strips – I think pepper skin is totally indigestible. (Red, yellow or orange peppers only please!

cooked Chinese duck	2 teaspoons soy sauce
pomelo	4 teaspoons Worcestershire sauce
packet beansprouts, trimmed then kept in iced water	
tablespoons light olive oil (not xtra-virgin)	250 g mixed leaf salad
	freshly ground black pepper
3–4 tablespoons rice vinegar	**serves 4**

These cold salad ingredients are served with warm duck. Buy a whole barbecued duck from Chinatown (don't let them chop it up), or use duck breasts as described in the variation. Pomelos can also be found in Chinese, Thai, or Vietnamese fruit shops. Like huge, dry-fleshed grapefruit, their segments stay together without losing their juice. If you can't find them, use a pink grapefruit instead. Eat this dish with chopsticks – the perfect salad-eating implements. In fact, they can be recommended for almost all salad-eating activities!

chinese duck salad

with pomelo and beansprouts

Slice the breasts off the duck in whole pieces. Put them, skin side down, on the work surface, then slice crossways in 3-cm strips. Set aside. Remove the crispy skin from the remaining duck, and cut into pieces about 3 cm square. Set aside. Shred the remaining duck meat into pieces as large as possible.

Pull the skin off the pomelo, then pull the membranes off each segment with your fingers (don't worry if they break – each one should be broken into 2 or 3 pieces anyway). Set aside. Drain the beansprouts.

Mix the olive oil, rice vinegar, soy sauce, pepper and Worcestershire sauce together, then divide between 4 big bowls. Add the leaves and turn them 3–4 times in the dressing until evenly coated. Add a pile of beansprouts, some shredded meat, then some breast and crispy skin. Top with the pomelo and serve.

Variation: No Chinese duck? Instead, char-grill 4 duck breasts until crispy in a stove-stop grill pan, then slice crossways and proceed as in the main recipe. Alternatively, marinate overnight in 125 ml rice vinegar mixed with 2 tablespoons soy sauce, 2 tablespoons fish sauce (Thai nam pla or Vietnamese nuoc mam) and 1 tablespoon chilli oil, then char-grill.

Thai salads are incredibly easy to make, and absolutely packed with flavour. Don't worry if you can't find all these ingredients — ring the changes according to whatever's available. I've used prawns, but you could use shredded barbecued pork, chicken or duck breast, for example. Rice vermicelli is like fine spaghetti: rice sticks like strappy fettuccine. Obviously, increase quantities for more servings.

1 tablespoon sesame seeds

1 bundle rice sticks or vermicelli

sprigs of coriander

your choice of

½ nashi pear, sliced lengthways

½ green mango or green papaya

½ baby cucumber

1 handful beansprouts, trimmed

2 fresh shiitake mushrooms

1 clump enokitake mushrooms

3 cherry tomatoes, halved

3 cooked tiger prawns, peeled

2.5 cm daikon (mooli), peeled and finely sliced

chilli dressing

1 teaspoon chilli oil

1 teaspoon fish sauce

2 teaspoons lime juice

1 teaspoon vegetable oil

½ teaspoon soy sauce

½ teaspoon sugar

serves 1

thai noodle salad
with shiitakes and chilli dressing

Stir-fry the sesame seeds in a dry frying pan for 1–2 minutes until golden. Set aside. Mix the dressing ingredients together in a small bowl or screw-top jar.

Put the rice stick or vermicelli noodles in a bowl and cover with boiling water for 3 minutes for vermicelli, or 10 minutes for rice sticks. Drain, rinse in cold water, then drain again, return to the bowl and cover with iced water and ice cubes. Drain just before serving.

Peel the mango or papaya with a vegetable peeler. Slice the flesh diagonally into strips. Cut the baby cucumber in half lengthways and scoop out the seeds. Peel, leaving strips of green. Slice finely diagonally. Remove and discard the stems from the shiitakes and slice the caps crossways into 4–6 pieces. Cut off and discard the roots from the enokitakes.

Tip the dressing into a big bowl, add the drained noodles, toss, then top with your choice of ingredients. Sprinkle with sesame seeds and coriander, and serve.

Simmer the sauce ingredients in a saucepan for 5 minutes, then chill. Cook the noodles according to the packet instructions, then drain, rinse in cold water and cool quickly over ice. Chill.

Put the shiitakes in a saucepan, cover with 250 ml boiling water and soak until soft. Remove and discard the mushroom stems. Add the soy sauce and mirin to the pan, bring to the boil and simmer for a few minutes until the liquid is slightly reduced. Cool and chill.

Poach the prawns in simmering salted water for about 1 minute until firm, then peel them, leaving the tail fins intact. Devein and split each prawn down the back to the fin, giving a butterfly shape. Chill.

Put the noodles in a bowl. Add ice cubes and top with the prawns, spring onions and mushrooms. Pour over the mushroom cooking liquid. Serve with separate dishes of wasabi paste and dipping sauce.

400 g soba noodles

12 dried shiitake mushrooms

2 tablespoons soy sauce

2 tablespoons mirin

12 uncooked prawns

12 spring onions, finely sliced

4 tablespoons wasabi paste

dipping sauce

250 ml dashi stock

125 ml Chinese rice wine or ginger wine

serves 4

Soba noodles are made from buckwheat. Firmer than other noodles, they are well suited to salad combinations. However other Japanese noodles are also delicious served cold. You could substitute white somen noodles, or the larger, ribbon-like udons. This salad is endlessly adaptable – you can omit the prawns and use sliced chicken or duck breast, poached fish (fresh or smoked), and some salad leaves. Mirin is Chinese rice wine – if unavailable, the alternative usually recommended is dry sherry, but I rather like ginger wine, which is both sweet and spicy. Dashi stock is available as a powder or concentrate in Asian shops and larger supermarkets.

japanese iced soba noodle salad

fresh pasta dough

250 g Italian flour, typo 00,
or plain flour

2 free-range eggs

2 free-range egg yolks

a pinch of salt

pesto and gorgonzola sauce

125 g Gorgonzola or Dolcellate
cheese, chopped

125 ml milk

75 ml double cream

25 g butter

4 tablespoons pesto, plus extra,
to serve

to serve

sprigs of basil

shavings of Parmesan cheese

sea salt and cracked
black pepper

serves 4

> A sinful combination of two very rich pasta sauces
> – and absolutely delicious! Make your own fresh pasta
> if you have a machine, otherwise buy dried pasta and
> cook according to the packet instructions.

fettuccine

with pesto and gorgonzola sauce

If making your own fresh pasta, put all the ingredients for the pasta dough into a food processor and work to a dough. Knead until the dough comes together, then roll through a pasta machine according to the manufacturer's instructions. Cut with the fettuccine attachment.

To make the sauce, melt the cheese in a saucepan with the milk, cream and butter, and cook, stirring, until the sauce is thickened (about 5 minutes).*

Cook the pasta in a large saucepan of salted water until al dente for dried pasta, or until it rises to the surface (about 1–2 minutes) for fresh pasta. Drain and divide between 4 big bowls. Spoon the sauce on top, then add an extra teaspoon of pesto and a sprig of basil to each one. Serve with the Parmesan shavings, some cracked pepper and a small dish of sea salt.

***Note:** The pesto can be stirred into the sauce at this point, or spooned on top of the pasta just before serving.

rice and beans

Simmer the pumpkin and potato, if using, in a saucepan until tender. Drain and mash with half the butter until creamy – it should have the consistency of thick soup (add a little milk if necessary).

Heat the oil and remaining butter in a frying pan, add the onions and sauté gently until soft and translucent. Add the garlic and cook until lightly golden (about 1–2 minutes). Add the rice and stir-fry for 1–2 minutes until the grains are well-covered with oil. Add a quarter of the stock and simmer gently, stirring, until absorbed. Repeat until all the stock has been used and the risotto is creamy and fluffy. Stir the pumpkin through the risotto and serve, topped with the Parmesan and deep-fried pumpkin crisps and chervil.

Note: To make pumpkin crisps, finely slice segments of pumpkin on a mandoline or with a vegetable peeler (include the skin). Deep-fry in vegetable oil until crispy. Drain on kitchen paper.

500 g peeled and deseeded pumpkin, cut into large chunks

4 potatoes, peeled and cut into large chunks (optional)

2 tablespoons butter

milk (optional – see method)

4 tablespoons olive oil

2 onions, finely chopped

2 fat garlic cloves, crushed

400 g risotto rice

1 litre boiling chicken stock

to serve

shavings of Parmesan cheese

pumpkin crisps (see note)

sprigs of chervil (optional)

serves 4

A Pacific-Rim version of Risotto al Zucca. Pumpkin is a much-loved vegetable in the Antipodes - roasted, puréed or souped. This is a variation on those cooking methods. As a pumpkin aficionado, I always use those with green or grey skins - they are drier and denser than the watery butternut kind, giving a more intense flavour and better texture.

pumpkin risotto

ful medames

with tabbouleh and egyptian flatbread

A simple, delicious Egyptian dish served as a starter or as a whole meal with wonderful Arab flatbreads: I like the huge ones, like giant pastry scarves. Hamine eggs are a traditional accompaniment — cooked for hours with onion skins, giving an unusual colour and texture. I prefer it without them, but a small side dish of quails' eggs is a happy compromise.

Soak the beans for 6–8 hours in cold water to cover. Drain the beans, put in a saucepan, cover with cold water, (do not salt), bring to the boil, skim, then reduce to a simmer and cook for 1 hour or until tender (the time will depend on the age of the beans). Drain. Meanwhile, put the garlic in a bowl, and mash with the oil, salt and pepper. Add the beans and toss well in the garlicky oil (the garlic taste will soften a little in the heat). Taste, and add extra sea salt and cracked pepper if needed. Fork through the chopped parsley and lemon juice and zest.

To make the tabbouleh, soak the buckwheat in water for 20 minutes, then drain. Skin, deseed and chop the tomatoes, and chop the parsley and mint. Put the tomatoes in a bowl with the buckwheat, chopped herbs, spring onions and cracked pepper. Sprinkle over the olive oil and lemon juice and toss well. Taste and adjust the seasoning.

To serve, put a large ladle of the ful medames in each of 4 big bowls, with a second large ladle of tabbouleh beside. Top with sprigs of parsley and lemon zest, then serve while the beans are still warm, together with large lacy Egyptian flatbreads and a dish of quails' eggs.

Variation: Ful medames and tabbouleh are delicious wrapped in the flatbread (sauced with hoummus), or in crisp cos lettuce leaves.

250 g dried ful (broad beans)

8 spring onions, sliced

2–4 garlic cloves, crushed

4 tablespoons olive oil

1 bunch of parsley, chopped

zest and juice of 1 lemon

sea salt and cracked pepper

tabbouleh

125 g toasted buckwheat

2 large ripe red tomatoes

1 bunch of flat leaf parsley

1 large bunch of mint

3 spring onions, sliced

2 tablespoons fruity olive oil

1 tablespoon lemon juice

sea salt and cracked pepper

to serve

sprigs of parsley

8 quails' eggs, boiled

Egyptian flatbread

serves 4

tortellone

with walnut sauce

This walnut sauce is wonderful with pasta, and it echoes the filling of the tortellone (make your own — or buy homemade ones from a good Italian deli). The sauce is very filling, so a little goes a long way — try it also as a stuffing for chicken breasts, or to top char-grilled steak.

tortellone

150 g ricotta cheese

4 tablespoons grated Parmesan cheese

125 g cooked, chopped spinach

10 basil leaves, torn

¼ teaspoon grated nutmeg

sea salt and freshly ground black pepper

1 quantity fresh pasta dough (page 34)

1 egg yolk, beaten

walnut sauce

2 tablespoons olive oil

2 garlic cloves, sliced

100 g fresh shelled walnuts, blanched and peeled*

2 cups chopped flat leaf parsley

125 g ricotta cheese

250 ml single cream or crème fraîche

salt and pepper

serves 4

To make the sauce, heat the oil in a small frying pan, and sauté the garlic for about 1 minute until golden. Whizz the walnuts, parsley, ricotta, cream, garlic and olive oil in a food processor. Just before serving, transfer to a saucepan and cook, stirring, for a few minutes until well heated and slightly thinned, adding extra water if needed.

To make the tortellone, make the pasta dough according to the recipe on page 34. Mix the ricotta, Parmesan, spinach, basil, nutmeg and seasonings in a bowl. Roll out the pasta dough, cut into circles around a small saucer, brush beaten egg around the edges and put 1–2 tablespoons of the ricotta mixture in the centre of each one. Fold over the pasta to make half circles, seal the edges, then turn them up like a hat brim and press the points together, sealing with more beaten egg.

Cook the tortellone in boiling salted water until they rise to the surface then cook 2 minutes more. Put 3–5 tortellone in each of 4 big bowls, top with the walnut sauce and serve.

*Note: the walnuts need not be blanched and peeled, but the flavour and colour will be vastly improved if they are. It's a little time-consuming, but the skinned walnuts can be frozen until you're ready to cook them.

moroccan harira soup

with chickpeas and lentils

Though described as a soup, this filling dish of chickpeas is really a stew, and is used to break the fast of Ramadan. Though usually made with lamb, I have omitted it for a great vegetarian treat.

100 g dried chickpeas

125 g yellow lentils or split peas (channa dhaal)

2 tablespoons unsalted butter

1 tablespoon olive oil

2 onions, grated

2 garlic cloves, crushed

2.5 cm fresh ginger, grated

1 cinnamon stick

1 teaspoon ground turmeric

500 ml crushed tomatoes, or 1 kg fresh tomatoes, skinned, deseeded and chopped

juice of 1 lemon

sea salt and cracked pepper

2 tablespoons beurre manié (optional) – see note

to serve

torn coriander leaves

8 boiled quails' eggs (optional)

serves 4

Soak the chickpeas for 6–8 hours in cold water to cover. Drain, put into a saucepan, cover with boiling (unsalted) water and simmer until tender – about 1 hour, but the time will depend on the age of the peas. Drain (reserve the water to use in the dish if you like).

Put the lentils or split peas in a saucepan, add 750 ml water, bring to the boil, reduce the heat and simmer for 15–20 minutes.

Heat the butter and oil in a frying pan, add the onions and sauté until soft and translucent. Add the garlic, ginger, cinnamon and turmeric and stir-fry for 5 minutes. Add 750 ml boiling water and simmer for 30 minutes. Add the lentils, chickpeas and tomatoes to the pan, stir well, then simmer for about 15 minutes to blend the flavours. Add the lemon juice and lots of cracked black pepper. Taste and adjust the seasoning with sea salt.

Serve in the big bowls, sprinkled with coriander leaves accompanied by a bowl of quails' eggs, if using.

Note: If necessary, you can thicken the sauce by stirring in 2 tablespoons beurre manié (1 tablespoon cornflour mashed together with 1 tablespoon butter). Cook for a few minutes until thickened.

Much of the flavour in prawns is in the shells, so cooking them unshelled releases the most marvellous flavour. In this Vietnamese-influenced dish, people peel their own prawns, so provide a big bowl for the debris and hot towels to help with the clean-ups. This is a hands-on dish!

char-grilled prawns
in chilli-lemongrass marinade

Heat 1 tablespoon of the oil in a small pan, add the garlic and cook for 1 minute until golden. Transfer to a wide shallow dish, then stir in another 2 tablespoons of the oil, plus the next 9 ingredients.

Rinse the prawns (not too long or you'll wash away the flavour). Push a toothpick into the prawn at the back of the neck, between the head and the shell and carefully prise out the dark vein (it should come out in one piece). Add the prawns to the dish and turn to coat. Set aside to marinate for 30 minutes.

Heat a stove-top grill pan, add the remaining oil and heat again. Add the prawns, in batches if necessary, and cook for about 3–5 minutes on each side until the shells turn red and the flesh becomes opaque all the way through (the time will depend on the size of the prawns).

Remove to heated bowls as they are ready. Serve with sprigs of coriander and grated lime zest. The fish sauce, lime wedges and a basket of hot towels should be served separately.

4 tablespoons corn or peanut oil

2 garlic cloves, crushed

6 red serrano chillies, very finely sliced

3 tablespoons fish sauce (*nam pla* or *nuoc mam*)

1 teaspoon salt

3 tablespoons rice vinegar

1 teaspoon sugar

6 kaffir lime leaves, finely sliced

3 stalks lemongrass, split lengthways and finely chopped

1 large onion, finely chopped

juice of 3 limes

about 250–500 g whole uncooked prawns per person

to serve

sprigs of coriander

grated kaffir lime zest

fish sauce (Thai *nam pla* or Vietnamese *nuoc mam*)

lime wedges

serves 4

ultry and meat

bengali fish curry

on basmati coconut rice

Bengal is renowned as one of the culinary capitals of India, a country in which every state has its own distinctive regional style, each as different as, for instance, those of France and Italy. Bengal is known for its use of aromatic mustard oil as a frying medium, especially for fish. If you can't find mustard oil (widely available in Asian markets) use corn oil and a little extra mustard seed to compensate. Don't use fine-flavoured or soft-fleshed fish for this recipe – the spices mean that you need a strong-flavoured, firm-fleshed fish like mullet or cod.

teaspoon salt

teaspoons ground turmeric

kg thick fish fillets, cut into pieces about 8–10 cm square

tablespoons mustard oil or corn oil

onions, cut in wedges through the root, separated into petals

tablespoon crushed garlic

.5 cm fresh ginger, grated

mild chilli, cored and sliced

cardamom pods, crushed

tablespoon mustard seeds

50 ml plain yoghurt

50 ml coconut milk

basmati coconut rice

cup basmati rice, washed in several changes of water

teaspoon salt

tablespoons coconut milk

sprigs of coriander, to serve

erves 4

Mix the salt and turmeric together and rub all over the fish. Heat the oil in a pan or wok and fry the fish for a few minutes on each side until almost cooked. Remove to a plate and keep them warm.

Add the onions and stir-fry gently until soft and translucent. Raise the heat and cook until lightly golden. Add the garlic and ginger and stir-fry until the garlic is cooked but not browned. Add the chilli, cardamom and mustard seeds. Stir-fry until the mustard seeds pop. Stir in the yoghurt and coconut milk, and heat gently without boiling. Add the fish and simmer gently for about 5 minutes until the fish is cooked through.

Meanwhile, put the rice in a saucepan with the salt, coconut milk and enough cold water to reach 1 finger's joint above the rice. Bring to the boil, put on the lid, reduce the heat and cook at a gentle simmer for about 12–15 minutes until the water is absorbed and the rice fluffy. Turn off the heat and leave the pan covered for 15 minutes more.

Divide the rice between 4 big bowls and place the pieces of fish on top. Spoon over the sauce and garnish with a sprig of coriander.

neapolitan seafood stew

A great dish with assertive flavours that remind me of wonderful holidays spent with my cousin in Naples. The fish market there has seafood so fresh it will bite you if you aren't careful, and the shellfish squirts water at you as you pass by. Alter the composition of this soup-stew according to what's available in your local market, but include thick white fish, shellfish and crustacea such as prawns.

4 large garlic cloves, crushed

1 bunch of thyme or rosemary

12 clams or other bivalves

12 mussels

about 4 tablespoons olive oil

2 large onions, cut into wedges through the root

8 ripe, very red tomatoes, skinned, halved and deseeded

1 kg thick boneless white fish fillets, such as cod

4–8 small whole fish, such as garfish, cleaned and scaled (optional)

8 uncooked prawns

1 litre boiling fish stock

sea salt and freshly ground black pepper

serves 4

Put 250 ml water in a saucepan with 1 crushed garlic clove and half the herbs, bring to the boil, then simmer to extract the flavours. Add the clams, cover with a lid and cook at a high heat, shaking the pan from time to time. Remove them as they open (about 1 minute) and put on a plate so they don't overcook. Add the mussels, cover with a lid and cook until they open. Remove as they do so and add to the clams. Taste the cooking stock, and if not too gritty, strain it through coffee filters into a cup and set aside.

Heat the oil in a large frying pan, add the onion wedges and cook until lightly browned on both sides. Reduce the heat and cook until softened. Stir in the remaining garlic and cook for a few minutes until golden. Add lots of freshly ground black pepper, then the tomatoes, remaining herbs, both kinds of fish and the prawns. Pour in the stock and heat just to boiling point. Reduce the heat and simmer for a few minutes until the fish turns opaque. Add the mussels, clams and the strained mussel poaching liquid, if using. Reheat and season to taste.

Divide between 4 big bowls. Serve with crusty Italian bread and a jug of light red wine or the peppery white wine from the Vesuvius area around the Bay of Naples.

Put the duck, skin side down, on a stove-top grill pan and cook at high heat until the fat begins to run. Reduce the heat to medium and add the sausages. Continue cooking, pouring off the fat from time to time, until the breast skin is crispy and the sausages are brown. Cook the other side, tipping off the fat from time to time.

Heat the oil in a flameproof casserole, add the garlic and cook 1 minute until golden. Add the tomatoes, herbs, duck and sausages, then enough stock to just cover the meat. Bring to the boil and simmer for about 35 minutes on top of the stove or in the oven. Remove the duck breasts and cut into 1 cm slices.

Cassoulets are perfect winter big bowl dishes. They always consist of beans and breadcrumbs baked with any number of meats. The traditional French dish from Toulouse should use a confit of goose or duck and the garlicky local sausage, but those I tasted in France went rather overboard on the beans and sausages. I felt a little cheated, so adapted the recipe for char-grilled duck breast. I think the traditional breadcrumbs taste like porridge and use an Italian gremolata instead. But if you would prefer the authentic taste, you can bake the dish topped with breadcrumbs.

Spread a layer of cooked beans over the bases of 4 ovenproof big bowls. Add a layer of sausages and sliced duck breasts, then an extra layer of beans to each. Boil down the stock until thickened, then pour into the big bowls, until the level of liquid is just below the top of the beans. Bake in a preheated oven at 200°C (400°F) Gas Mark 6 for 35 minutes or until crusty and light brown.*

Mix the gremolata ingredients together, sprinkle over the top of each bowl and serve. A light salad is the only accompaniment you need.

*Note: Alternatively, you can cook the cassoulet in a large casserole and serve in the big bowls.

2 large barbary duck breasts

4 coarse Italian pork sausages or Toulouse sausages

2 tablespoons olive oil

4 garlic cloves, crushed

200 ml crushed tomatoes

a bouquet garni of fresh thyme, bay leaves and parsley

boiling chicken stock (see method)

dried haricot or butter beans, soaked 6–8 hours, then cooked without salt until tender

gremolata

4 tablespoons chopped parsley

1 garlic clove, crushed

grated rind of 1 lemon

serves 4

big bowl cassoulet
with char-grilled duck breasts and toulouse sausages

carbonade of beef

with mushrooms and mashed potatoes

This is a beef-in-beer dish from northern France and Belgium, with a glorious gravy just made for the big bowl treatment. It's perfect with big flat field mushrooms thickly sliced and sautéed in butter or olive oil, plus lots of lovely mustard mashed potatoes to mop up the juices. The original recipe would use butter to cook the beef, but I prefer olive oil. Use either, or a mixture of both. It's also traditional to serve this dish with slices of fried toast, but I much prefer mashed potatoes — please yourself!

Cut the meat in large 5 cm cubes. Heat the olive oil in a flameproof casserole and brown the meat very well, in batches, removing them to a dish as they brown. Pour any juices into the dish of meat, add the onions to the casserole (with a little more olive oil, if necessary) and cook gently until softened, translucent and lightly browned. Add the garlic and stir-fry for a couple of minutes until golden. Push the garlic and onions to the side of the casserole with a slotted spoon. Sprinkle the flour over the oil in the pan and cook, stirring, until browned (make sure there aren't any white bits, or they will be lumps later). Tip the meat and the juices back into the pan, add the tomatoes, beer and herbs, bring to the boil, reduce to a simmer and cook, covered, on top of the stove or in a low oven for 2–3 hours.

Cool and chill, preferably overnight. One hour before serving, remove and discard the fat from the surface, then reheat gently on top of the stove or in the oven at 200°C (400°F) Gas Mark 6.

Meanwhile, sauté the mushrooms in a little butter and oil and prepare the mashed potatoes. To serve, divide the mashed potatoes between 4 big bowls, spoon in the meat beside the potatoes and top with the sautéed mushrooms.

Pour the hot stock carefully down the sides of the big bowls, then serve.

1.5 kg braising beef

2–4 tablespoons olive oil

2 large onions, finely sliced

2 garlic cloves, crushed

2–3 tablespoons plain flour

125 ml puréed tomatoes

500 ml Belgian-style beer (lager)

3 fresh bay leaves

1 bunch of thyme

sea salt and cracked pepper

to serve

sautéed mushrooms

creamy mashed potatoes

serves 4

lamb tagine

with honey and quinces

Autumn quinces give wonderful scent to this Moroccan tagine. At other times of the year, substitute apples or even firm pears. I don't usually like honey or fruit with meat, but this tagine is an utterly delicious exception.

4 tablespoons olive oil

1.5 kg lamb neck fillet, cut in big chunks (other cuts of meat will also work well)

2 onions, grated

3 tablespoons chopped parsley

2.5 cm fresh ginger, grated

1 cinnamon stick

1 pinch saffron threads, soaked in boiling water to cover for 20 minutes, or 2 sachets powder

2 quinces, 3 pears or 3 apples, peeled, quartered and cored

3 tablespoons honey

salt and pepper

sprigs of coriander, to serve

pistachio couscous

450 g easy-cook couscous

1.25 litres boiling stock or water

4 tablespoons shelled pistachio nuts

2 tablespoons pine nuts

1 tablespoon butter

serves 4

Heat the oil in a flameproof casserole, add the meat and sauté until browned. Add the onions, parsley, ginger, cinnamon, saffron and enough boiling water to cover by about 1 cm. Return to the boil, skim, reduce to a bare simmer and cook for about 1 hour, or until tender.

Remove the meat to a plate. Add the fruit, honey, salt, pepper and 250 ml boiling water to the pan. Simmer until tender (a few minutes for pears and apples, longer for quinces, which will turn pink)

Return the meat to the pan, cover and simmer for a further 15 minutes.

Meanwhile, put the couscous in a heatproof bowl, pour over boiling stock or water and put in the oven to keep warm until all the liquid is absorbed. Blanch the pistachios and pop them out of their skins (so they're bright green). Dry-toast the pine nuts in a frying pan until golden (about 30 seconds). Stir the butter through the couscous, fluffing up the grains with a fork, then stir in the nuts.

Pile the couscous into the big bowls, spoon the tagine around and top with sprigs of coriander.

There is much discussion amongst aficionados about the precise composition of Irish stew. Some insist on carrots, others regard them as anathema. I like to use waxy yellow potatoes rather than the white floury kind, because they don't melt into the stock. The cloudy stock tastes wonderful, but I always think it looks a bit grim. This recipe keeps the stock clear and golden. I like to use big chunks of lamb, not the mimsy little bits you see in most recipes. That way the meat is much more succulent.

irish stew

Heat the oil or butter in a flameproof casserole and brown the onion wedges on both sides. Transfer to a plate. Add the lamb to the casserole and fry in batches until browned on all sides. Add the chicken stock, wine and seasoning. Bring to the boil, cover, reduce to a simmer and cook for 30–35 minutes. Remove from the heat, cool and chill in the casserole, preferably overnight.

2 tablespoons corn oil or butter

3 large onions, cut into 6 wedges through the root

1.5 kg lamb neck fillet or similar stewing lamb, cut into large (about 5 cm) chunks

600 ml boiling chicken stock

300 ml white wine

1 kg small waxy yellow potatoes, peeled

3 large carrots, sliced thickly, or 12 baby carrots

1 celery stalk, finely diced

beurre manié (1 tablespoon unsalted butter mashed with 1 tablespoon plain flour) – optional

1 bunch of parsley, chopped

sea salt and cracked pepper

serves 4

About 1 hour before serving, remove and discard the fat off the top, add the potatoes, carrots and celery to the casserole and simmer until the vegetables are tender. Stir in the beurre manié, if using, cook until lightly thickened, then taste and adjust the seasoning. To serve, divide between 4 big bowls, pour the stock over, sprinkle with parsley and serve with chunks of soda bread and glasses of Guinness.

Variation:
scandinavian fishermen's stew

Interestingly – a stew made with beef, not fish. Perhaps the sailors get bored with fish! Substitute braising steak for the lamb, then remove it, and cook the onions in the same pan until soft and translucent. Thinly slice all the potatoes, put half in the base of a flameproof casserole, with the meat and onions on top. Add the remaining potatoes and seasoning. Pour 600 ml lager-style beer on top, bring to the boil, cover and cook at a gentle simmer on top of the stove or in a low oven for about 1½ hours. Transfer the meat and vegetables to 4 big bowls, skim the fat off the pan juices and pour the juice into the bowls. Serve with Danish beer and rye bread.

westphalian braised pork

with baby potatoes and smoked bacon

A deceptively simple recipe named for the former princely state of Westphalia on the North Sea coast of Germany — famous for the quality of its pork products. If the potatoes are very small, such as Ratte or Pink Fir Apples, leave them whole.

1.5 kg small waxy potatoes, pink or yellow if possible, peeled and halved lengthways if large

3 onions, cut into wedges through the root

about 8 slices smoked bacon (enough to cover the base of your casserole), rinds removed

4 large or 8 small free-range pork chops

600 ml crème fraîche

125 ml white wine

125 ml white vermouth

1 cinnamon stick

50 g butter, diced

6 sprigs of thyme, plus extra, to serve

freshly ground black pepper

serves 4

Line the base of a flameproof casserole with slices of smoked bacon. Add a layer of the onions and potatoes, then arrange the pork chops on top. Pour in the crème fraîche, followed by the white wine and white vermouth. Tuck the cinnamon stick in the middle, then add a couple of large sprigs of thyme and lots of freshly ground black pepper.

Bring to the boil, immediately reduce the heat, cover with a lid, then simmer at the lowest possible heat (use a heat-diffusing mat if necessary) for about 1 hour, or until the meat is falling off the bone. (Do not allow the liquid to boil, or the meat will be tough and the cream will separate.)

Transfer the meat to 4 big bowls, add a share of the bacon, onions and potatoes, then strain the stock over the top. Add sprigs of thyme and serve.

If preferred, the pork can be sliced into bite-sized pieces and the dish served with a large soup spoon. Chunks of crusty French bread and a crisp white wine or lager are suitable accompaniments.

Vary the vegetables in this curry depending on what's good in the market, as a local cook would in Jamaica. Just try to avoid using butternut squash instead of real grey-or-green skinned pumpkin – it has rather watery flesh, and is a waste of time to a real pumpkin-lover! If you leave out the bacon, this curry is a gorgeous, spicy treat for vegetarians.

spicy caribbean vegetable curry

with crispy smoked bacon

Heat 1 tablespoon corn oil in a pan, add the bacon or pancetta, if using, and cook until crispy. Remove from the pan, drain on kitchen paper and set aside.

Heat the remaining oil in the pan, add the chilli, cinnamon, cloves and seeds from the cardamom pods, and stir-fry until you cough – that means the flavours have been released. Add the onion wedges and cook until well softened and slightly browned. Turn and cook the other side. Remove and set aside.

Add your choice of the pumpkin, sweet potatoes, plantain, choko or aubergines and turn until well coated with the spices. Add the stock and cook until almost done. Add the pattypans or courgettes, if using and cook for 2 minutes. Add the sugarsnaps and cook for another 2 minutes. Pour in the coconut milk and bring to just below boiling (take care or the milk will split). Add the prepared mini red peppers, if using, and reserved onions, cover with a lid, and remove from the heat.

Divide the rice between 4 heated big bowls, add the vegetables and sauce, and top with the crispy bacon, if using.

2 tablespoons corn oil

125 g smoked bacon or pancetta, snipped into strips (optional)

½ Scotch bonnet chilli, deseeded and sliced

1 cinnamon stick

3 cloves

6 green cardamom pods

1 red onion, cut into wedges through the root

500 ml chicken stock

500 ml coconut milk

boiled rice, to serve

your choice of

250 g pumpkin chunks

2 orange sweet potatoes, cut in chunks

1 plantain, peeled and sliced diagonally

1 choko (chayote), diced

8 round yellow aubergines

8 pattypan squash or 4 small courgettes

125 g sugarsnap peas

6 mini or 2 large red peppers, charred, peeled and deseeded

serves 4

This traditional sweet-but-savoury Thai concoction is amazingly easy to construct, and its garnishes can be added or subtracted according to whatever interesting ingredients you have to hand. However, there are a few you simply must have: coriander, spring onions, a chilli or two, and a Thai curry paste – this one is the milder orange mussaman (Muslim) paste.

4 bundles rice vermicelli noodles

corn oil, for deep-frying

garnishes

1 tablespoon corn oil

1 tablespoon Thai chilli paste, such as mussaman

4 pork chops, boned and sliced

4–8 uncooked prawns, peeled and split lengthways if large

1–4 chillies, finely sliced

8 spring onions, finely sliced

1 bunch of coriander

sweet thai sauce

125 ml rice vinegar

100 g palm sugar or dark muscovado sugar

4 tablespoons soy sauce

4 tablespoons fish sauce

serves 4

crisp thai noodles

with chillies, pork and prawns

To make the sauce, put the vinegar, sugar, soy and fish sauce in a small pan and cook, stirring until dissolved. Set aside to keep warm.

To prepare the garnishes, heat the oil in a frying pan, add the Thai chilli paste and cook until you cough (about 1–2 minutes). Add the pork strips and stir-fry until crispy. Add the prawns and stir-fry for 1 minute. Transfer to a dish and keep them warm. Stir-fry the chillies and spring onions for 1 minute, then add to the prawns and pork.

To prepare the noodles, line 4 heated big bowls with crumpled kitchen paper, then fill a wok one-third full of corn oil and heat over a high heat to 190°C (375°F). To test, drop a fragment of noodle into the oil: the oil is hot enough when the noodle immediately puffs and curls. Add a bundle of noodles – they will puff up immediately. Let cook for 1 minute or until light gold then, using tongs, carefully turn it over and cook the other side. Remove the noodles and put in one of the bowls. Repeat with the other 3 bundles (take care to reheat the oil and skim off any debris between batches).

When all bundles are cooked, turn them over in the bowls and discard the paper. Put the pork, prawns, spring onions and chillies on top of the noodles. Pour over the sweet hot dressing, and top with coriander sprigs. Serve immediately with chopsticks.

index